TO EVERY DOG
THERE IS A SEASON

FUN LESSONS FOR LIFE

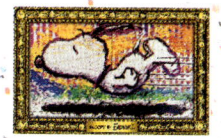

LEARN
FROM THE MISTAKES OF OTHERS; YOU DON'T HAVE ENOUGH TIME TO MAKE THEM ALL YOURSELF!

To Every Dog There Is A Season: Spring

IF AT FIRST
YOU DO SUCCEED—
TRY TO HIDE YOUR
ASTONISHMENT.

Harry F. Banks

It is the simplest
things—not the great
occasions—that in
retrospect give off
the greatest glow
of happiness.

Bob Hope

Thank God for normal
days. There are far
too few of them.

Gloria Gaither

ANYBODY WHO KNOWS EVERYTHING SHOULD BE TOLD A THING OR TWO.

Franklin P. Jones

A WELL-INFORMED PERSON IS SOMEBODY WHO HAS THE SAME VIEWS AND OPINIONS AS YOURS.

ENCOURAGEMENT IS AWESOME. IT HAS THE CAPACITY...TO ACTUALLY CHANGE THE COURSE OF ANOTHER HUMAN BEING'S DAY, WEEK, OR LIFE.

Charles R. Swindoll

NEVER PUT OFF UNTIL TOMORROW WHAT YOU CAN AVOID ALTOGETHER.

ONE OF THE GREATEST LABOR-SAVING INVENTIONS OF TODAY IS TOMORROW.

Vincent T. Goss

SINCE LIGHT TRAVELS FASTER THAN SOUND, IS THAT WHY SOME PEOPLE APPEAR BRIGHT UNTIL YOU HEAR THEM SPEAK?

A WORD FITLY SPOKEN IS LIKE APPLES OF GOLD IN SETTING OF SILVER.

The Book of Proverbs

DIPLOMACY—THE ART OF LETTING SOMEONE HAVE YOUR WAY.

A SINGLE FACT CAN SPOIL A GOOD ARGUMENT.

No Way Out

IS SO BIG OR SO COMPLICATED THAT IT CAN'T BE RUN AWAY FROM.

Linus

A PERSON'S MIND, ONCE STRETCHED BY A NEW IDEA, NEVER REGAINS ITS ORIGINAL DIMENSIONS.

Oliver Wendell Holmes

MY MIND NOT ONLY WANDERS, SOMETIMES IT LEAVES COMPLETELY.

THE CHIEF FUNCTION OF YOUR BODY IS TO CARRY YOUR BRAIN AROUND.

IF YOU CAN LEARN TO LAUGH IN SPITE OF THE CIRCUMSTANCES, YOU WILL ENRICH OTHERS, ENRICH YOURSELF, AND MORE THAN THAT, YOU WILL LAST!

Barbara Johnson

SWALLOW YOUR PRIDE OCCASIONALLY—YOU'LL FIND IT'S NON-FATTENING.

LIFE IS WHAT WE MAKE IT, ALWAYS HAS BEEN, ALWAYS WILL BE.

Grandma Moses

TO EVERYTHING THERE IS A SEASON, A TIME TO EVERY PURPOSE UNDER THE HEAVEN.

The Book of Ecclesiastes

LAUGH AT YOURSELF,
BEFORE ANYONE ELSE CAN.

Elsa Maxwell

YOU GROW UP THE DAY
YOU HAVE YOUR FIRST
REAL LAUGH—AT YOURSELF.

Ethel Barrymore

THAT'S THE SECRET TO LIFE...REPLACE ONE WORRY WITH ANOTHER.

Charles Schulz

HE WHO LEARNS AND RUNS AWAY, LIVES TO LEARN ANOTHER DAY.

Henry David Thoreau

To Every Dog There Is A Season: Summer

ADVENTURE
IS WORTHWHILE
IN ITSELF.

Amelia Earhart

It isn't the big pleasures that count the most; it's making a great deal out of the little ones.

Jean Webster

Where your treasure is, there will your heart be also.

The Book of Matthew

WHEN SOMEONE IS HAVING A BAD DAY, BE SILENT, SIT CLOSE BY, AND NUZZLE THEM GENTLY.

LONELINESS ISN'T SUCH A BAD THING, EXCEPT WHEN YOU DON'T HAVE ANYONE TO SHARE IT WITH.

Barbara Johnson

HARD WORK NEVER KILLED ANYBODY, BUT WHY TAKE A CHANCE?

Charlie McCart

EAT DESSERT FIRST! AFTER ALL, LIFE IS UNCERTAIN.

NEVER CRITICIZE YOUR HAIR CUTTER—AT LEAST NOT WHILE YOURS IS THE HAIR BEING CUT.

YOU CAN OBSERVE A LOT BY WATCHING.

Yogi Berra

HUMOR HELPS US TO OVERLOOK THE UNBECOMING, UNDERSTAND THE UNCONVENTIONAL, TOLERATE THE UNPLEASANT, OVERCOME THE UNEXPECTED, AND OUTLAST THE UNBEARABLE.

Billy Graham

GIVE WHAT YOU HAVE.
TO SOMEONE IT MAY BE
BETTER THAN YOU DARE
TO THINK.

Longfellow

BE KIND TO UNKIND
PEOPLE. IT GETS TO
THEM.

Undercover in Hollywood

ADMIT

YOUR ERRORS
BEFORE SOMEONE ELSE
EXAGGERATES THEM.

ONLY SOME OF US LEARN BY OTHER PEOPLE'S MISTAKES; THE REST OF US HAVE TO BE THE OTHER PEOPLE.

EXPERIENCE IS SOMETHING YOU DON'T GET UNTIL JUST AFTER YOU NEED IT.

YOU LEARN MORE BY LISTENING (YOU ALREADY KNOW WHAT YOU WOULD SAY).

BEWARE OF THE HALF TRUTH. YOU MAY HAVE GOTTEN HOLD OF THE WRONG HALF.

THROW YOUR HEART OUT
IN FRONT OF YOU. AND
RUN AHEAD TO CATCH IT.

Arab Proverb

DREAMS COME A SIZE
TOO BIG SO THAT WE
CAN GROW INTO THEM.

Josie Bisset

WHEN I WAS GROWING UP I ALWAYS WANTED TO BE SOMEONE. NOW I REALIZE I SHOULD HAVE BEEN MORE SPECIFIC.

Lily Tomlin

ALWAYS REMEMBER YOU'RE UNIQUE, JUST LIKE EVERYONE ELSE.

WE ARE LOSING OUR MINDS...LITTLE PIECES OF MIND CALLED NEURONS FLY OUT OF OUR HEADS DAILY IN LARGE NUMBERS...IT DOESN'T HELP TO WEAR A HAT.

THERE ARE THREE KINDS OF PEOPLE: THOSE WHO CAN COUNT AND THOSE WHO CAN'T.

THERE'S NOTHING WRONG WITH HAVING NOTHING TO SAY, AS LONG AS YOU DON'T SAY IT OUT LOUD.

To Every Dog There Is A Season: Fall

EXPERIENCE

IS THAT MARVELOUS THING THAT ENABLES YOU TO RECOGNIZE A MISTAKE WHEN YOU MAKE IT AGAIN.

ALWAYS DO RIGHT—THIS WILL GRATIFY SOME AND ASTONISH THE REST.

Mark Twain

ABOVE ALL ELSE, GUARD YOUR HEART, FOR IT IS THE WELLSPRING OF LIFE.

The Book of Proverbs

SUNSHINE IS A MATTER OF ATTITUDE.

F. W. Boreham

LOOK FOR THE LIGHT BEHIND EVERY SHADOW.

Dr. Robert Schuller

YOU ARE ONLY AS WISE AS OTHERS PERCEIVE YOU TO BE.

M. Shawn Cole

THE DIFFERENCE BETWEEN
THE RIGHT WORD AND
THE ALMOST RIGHT WORD
IS THE DIFFERENCE
BETWEEN LIGHTNING AND
THE LIGHTNING BUG.

Mark Twain

NO ONE IS LISTENING
UNTIL YOU MAKE A
MISTAKE.

NEVER EAT MORE THAN
YOU CAN LIFT.

Miss Piggy

WHAT YOU EAT STANDING
UP DOESN'T COUNT.

Beth Barnes

HOT FUDGE FILLS DEEP NEEDS.

Susan Isaacs

ONE OF THE SECRETS OF A HAPPY LIFE IS CONTINUOUS SMALL TREATS.

Iris Murdoch

From Sir With Love

IT IS FAR

MORE IMPRESSIVE
WHEN OTHERS DISCOVER
YOUR GOOD QUALITIES
WITHOUT YOUR HELP.

IF WE GIVE SOMEONE A
PIECE OF BREAD AND
BUTTER, THAT'S KINDNESS,
BUT IF WE PUT JELLY OR
PEANUT BUTTER ON IT,
THEN IT'S LOVING
KINDNESS.

Barbara Johnson

DO TO OTHERS AS YOU
WOULD HAVE THEM
DO TO YOU.

The Book of Luke

ONLY A LIFE IN THE
SERVICE OF OTHERS IS
WORTH LIVING.

Albert Einstein

THE TROUBLE WITH DOING SOMETHING RIGHT THE FIRST TIME IS THAT NOBODY APPRECIATES HOW DIFFICULT IT WAS.

GETTING THINGS ACCOMPLISHED ISN'T NEARLY AS IMPORTANT AS TAKING TIME FOR LOVE.

Janette Oke

THE SECRET OF SUCCESS
IS TO STAY COOL AND
CALM ON TOP AND
PADDLE LIKE CRAZY
UNDERNEATH.

IF YOU REMAIN CALM,
YOU JUST DON'T HAVE
ALL THE FACTS.

TRY READING THE HANDWRITING ON THE WALL BEFORE YOUR BACK IS UP AGAINST IT.

LIFE IS LIKE AN ICE-CREAM CONE: JUST WHEN YOU THINK YOU'VE GOT IT LICKED, IT DRIPS ALL OVER YOU!

SUCCESS ALWAYS OCCURS IN PRIVATE, AND FAILURE IN FULL VIEW.

IF AT FIRST YOU DON'T SUCCEED, SEE IF THE LOSER GETS ANYTHING.

To Every Dog There Is A Season: Winter

IF YOU
THINK NO ONE CARES ABOUT YOU, TRY MISSING A FEW PAYMENTS.

THE BEST WAY TO FORGET
ALL YOUR TROUBLES IS
TO WEAR TIGHT SHOES.

HAPPINESS IS FOUND
ALONG THE WAY, NOT AT
THE END OF THE
JOURNEY.

ALWAYS BE OPEN TO THE MIRACLE OF THE SECOND CHANCE.

Rev. David Stier

WHEN YOU GET TO THE END OF YOUR ROPE, TIE A KNOT AND HANG ON—AND THEN SWING!

IF I TRAVELED TO THE END
   OF THE RAINBOW
AS DAME FORTUNE DID INTEND,
MURPHY WOULD BE THERE
   TO TELL ME
THE POT'S AT THE
   OTHER END.

                              Bert Whitney

IF YOU CAN COUNT YOUR MONEY, YOU DON'T HAVE A BILLION DOLLARS.

J. Paul Getty

A PENNY SAVED IS NOT NEARLY ENOUGH.

IF WE DID THE THINGS WE ARE CAPABLE OF, WE WOULD ASTOUND OURSELVES.

Thomas Edison

YOU MAY NOT KNOW ALL THE ANSWERS, BUT YOU PROBABLY WON'T BE ASKED ALL THE QUESTIONS EITHER.

IT'S OKAY TO RELAX.
IT'S ESSENTIAL!

Charles R. Swindoll

I'VE GOT ALL THE MONEY I'LL EVER NEED...IF I DIE BY FOUR O'CLOCK.

Henny Youngman

As The Sun Sets Slowly In The West, We Bid You A Fine Farewell

FOR FAST
ACTING RELIEF, TRY SLOWING DOWN.

Lily Tomlin

TO EVERY DOG THERE IS A SEASON
FUN LESSONS FOR LIFE

Bright, expressive paintings by Tom Everhart, the only artist authorized by Charles Schulz to illustrate Peanuts characters, are paired with lighthearted, fun-loving sentiments in this celebration of life.

Artwork copyright © 1999 UFS
Design by Lecy Design
Text copyright © 1999 FrontPorch Books,
a division of Garborg's, LLC

Published by Garborg's, LLC
P. O. Box 20132, Bloomington, MN 55420

All rights reserved.
No part of this book may be reproduced
in any form without permission in writing
from the publisher.

ISBN 1-58375-468-7

Printed in Mexico